BEIRUT

Alan Bowne

BROADWAY PLAY PUBLISHING INC
56 E 81st St., NY NY 10028-0202
212 772-8334 fax: 212 772-8358
http://www.BroadwayPlayPubl.com

BEIRUT
© Copyright 1985 by Alan Bowne

First printing: March 1988
This printing: February 2004
I S B N: 0-88145-057-X

Book design: Marie Donovan
Word processing: Microsoft Word for Windows
Typographic controls: Ventura Publisher 2.0 P E
Typeface: Palatino
Printed and bound in the U S A

for
Michael D'Apice
Brooklyn Boy

BEIRUT originally was workshopped at the Bay Area Playwrights Festival, Mill Valley, CA, in August 1986. Alma Becker directed the production.

BEIRUT received its first Off-Off Broadway production by the Manhattan Class Company at the Nat Horne Theatre in New York City on 23 March 1987, with the following cast and creative contributors:

TORCH . . . . Michael David Morrison
BLUE . . . . Marisa Tomei
GUARD . . . . Terry Rabine

Director . . . . Jimmy Bohr
Set design . . . . Elizabeth Doyle
Lighting . . . . John Hastings
Stage manager . . . . Georgette Lewis

The Off-Broadway premiere of BEIRUT, produced by
Barbara Darwal, Peter von Mayrhauser, Maggie Lear,
Janet Robinson, and Harold Thau, was presented at
the Westside Arts Theater in New York City. It opened
9 June 1987, with the following cast and creative
contributors:

TORCH . . . . Michael David Morrison
BLUE . . . . Laura San Giacomo
GUARD . . . . Terry Rabine

Director . . . . Jimmy Bohr
Set design . . . . .Elizabeth Doyle
Lighting . . . . John Hastings
Costumes . . . . Walker Hicklin
Stage manager . . . . Laura Kravets

CHARACTERS & SETTING

TORCH, *a good-looking streety male in his early twenties*
BLUE, *a bright, pretty, sensuous female in her early twenties*
GUARD, *with flashlight*

Time: The near future. Night.

*A bare, shabby, one-room basement apartment in an
abandoned building on the Lower East Side of Manhattan. A
crumby sofabed, thin mattress with dirty sheets and pillows.
A clock radio. Papers, medical journals, canned goods, and
various trash on floor. A sink. Stairs leading down from
elevated entrance door. One window with tattered shade.*

*NOTE: The style of orthography employed throughout is
intentional. So are the bad grammar and odd punctuation.
The idiom employed is New York City street. Periods within
lines do not indicate full stops but serve, rather, as rhythmic
breathing notes. Absence of punctuation indicates that the
line should be read in one breath.*

(Darkness)

(Lights dimly up on a human form wadded among the dirty sheets on the mattress)

(Clock radio snaps on; lighting up.)

RADIO D J: *(Voiceover)* ...and this is so old it has hair on it! It's for Skull and his pals out in Flatbush. This one's for you, Skull!

(The refrain of the song, "We Are the World", blasts forth.)

(A man's hand rises from the wadded sheets and slams down onto the radio, cutting it off.)

(Groggily, TORCH sits up edge of bed, covering his nakedness with a sheet. He lights a candle next to bed.)

(Lights up)

(TORCH, in sheet, crosses to sink. Drops sheet, revealing a large "P" tattooed on his left buttock. Throws water on his face.)

(Turning from sink, he rummages in trash for undershorts and slips them on. Squatting, he searches for a can in debris. Can opener. Punches hole in concentrated milk can, drinks. Removes lid from can of tuna and eats hungrily, licking fingers.)

(A siren sounds. TORCH leaps to window, lifts shade, looks out. A flashing light beam stabs him in eyes. Turning from window, he retrieves sheet and huddles on mattress. Hears something. Springs to feet. Stealthily crosses to stairs.)

TORCH: *(In a loud whisper, directed up stairs at entrance door)* Blue? That ain't you, is it?

(No response)

(Despairingly, he crosses back to mattress. Plops down. Flicks on radio, twiddling dial: Strauss's "Zarathustra".)

(As the music plays:)

(The young man begins to caress his body, staring up at the ceiling. Gradually his hands work down to his privates, which he fondles in his shorts. Rolls onto stomach. Slowly begins humping mattress. Suddenly: quick rapping at entrance door. TORCH sits up at once, snapping off radio.)

TORCH: Blue?

(Repeat rapping. TORCH, excited, apprehensive, springs across room and up the stairs to the entrance door. Yanks open door, admits BLUE. They stare for an instant. She is wearing a drab, shapeless dress over soiled sneakers and is carrying a large purse. Delightedly, she dashes down steps as TORCH, after a quick look at landing, closes door and turns to look dazedly at girl.)

BLUE: So lock it.

TORCH: You can't lock it.

BLUE: When's the next patrol?

TORCH: Three A M.

BLUE: OK, we got a few hours.

TORCH: Suckhead! Comin' here. *(Goes down stairs, crosses to window, peers out.)* The whole Lower East's a quarantine zone for doofases who test positive. And you, a negative, send me this fuckfanny underground message that says, "I'm comin' in." Get it through your head, Blue. I'm in quarantine. That's K-U—

BLUE: *(Cutting him off, dropping purse on floor.)* Don't I get a kiss?

TORCH: Fuckin' you know I can't kiss you.

BLUE: *(Approaching him.)* A hug at least?

(He looks into her eyes for a beat. Then grasps her head in his hands, fearful of too much contact, but passionately, touching her forehead to his chest. Abruptly pushes her away.)

TORCH: O K. So there it is. *(Plops onto mattress, wrapping himself in sheet)* That was worth risking your life, or what?

BLUE: It was worth it.

TORCH: How'd you the fuck get in here?

BLUE: F D R Drive. Overpass at East Sixth.

TORCH: When?

BLUE: Early this morning. I holed up in that abandoned building across the street until dark. All day I kept peeking out to see if you'd come to the window.

TORCH: What'd you do, bribe somebody to find me? That's dangerous!

BLUE: Bribes? Your muthah takes bribes. *(Looking around)* You know, I think I liked it better in that bomb site across the street. They put you in *here*?

TORCH: They're runnin' outa places. Least I'm alone here.

BLUE: How long they gonna keep you?

TORCH: 'Till get... lesions.

BLUE: And then what?

TORCH: Then I dunno. Once you got symptoms, they put you someplace else.

BLUE: You got any?

TORCH: I dunno.

BLUE: Can I look?

TORCH: *No! (Wraps sheet tighter about himself.)* Wasn't so cocksuckin' hot I would be covered wit' clothes. Hate to be naked even. Fraid of what I'll see.

BLUE: Torch, I wanna look.

TORCH: Hey! They got a Lesion Patrol for this. They'll be here at three. I'll send you a medical report, O K?

BLUE: *(Stirring cans on floor with foot)* You eating right?

(No response)

BLUE: Hey! Blood-positive does *not* mean! You'll come down with it.

TORCH: Chances are I will. Tomorrow. Next year. I could be here. A long time.

BLUE: You look good.

(Beat)

TORCH: Sodoyou.

BLUE: *(Indicating dress.)* In this? They got everybody in burlap bags out there. *(Starts picking up trash.)* You can go to prison for being "provocative." Calvin Klein's got a reprise of the moo-moo, are you ready? *(Looks up at ceiling.)* It's weird. No sex detectors. God, I am so sick of those little cameras everywhere. *(Twirls)* It's like you're free!

TORCH: They don't care if positives fuck! If you're good as dead, you can fuck like a Sicilian.

BLUE: Shut up. You're not dead.

TORCH: I get *notes* under my door. Girls, guys. "'P' is for positive, we're both Ps, so what the hell?"

BLUE: You must want to.

(TORCH rises from mattress and, swathed in the sheet, crosses to window. Peeks out.)

TORCH: They say! That repeated reinfectionals *(Pronounce as written)* by this thing? Could bring it on. And just yesterday, I look out in that shitty lot over there? And there's this P-guy. Fuckin' some P-slut! Onna broken wall. Broad daylight.

BLUE: *(Shrugging)* She was probably a prostitute. Every hooker in New York's in here.

TORCH: And negatives sneak in here and fuck 'em too!

BLUE: Well, they can't fuck out there. Sex is a capital crime!

TORCH: *(Turning from window.)* Good! If they stop people boffin', this'll stop. I can't *believe* these stupids, comin' in here and getting infected. This neighborhood's called Beirut for a good reason!

BLUE: I came to Beirut. Am I a stupid?

(Beat)

TORCH: But you. Ain't gettin'. Infected.

BLUE: What's the difference? If I'm caught in here, they'll shoot me.

TORCH: *(Anxious)* But you can get out again?

BLUE: Sure, same way I got in. *(Sits on haunches on bed.)* There's six guys. Hung from lampposts. On 14th Street.

TORCH: There's what?

BLUE: Six blood-negatives. Who were caught in here. Hung by their necks. As a warning.

TORCH: But that's unsanitary!

BLUE: They mean business.

TORCH: *(Stunned)* Jesus. *(Turns away, quickly turns back)* Good! Crime does not pay! *(Suddenly worried)* You can't stay long, Blue. Give yourself plenny time to get out.

BLUE: I won't get stretched, even if I'm caught. God, it is so shining hot. *(She pulls dress over head. She is in bra and panties.)*

TORCH: *(Staring)* The fuck are you doin?

(BLUE sprawls across bed, on her stomach, hugging pillow, twining legs seductively.)

BLUE: Check it out.

TORCH: *I ast you a question!*

BLUE: Cost me plenty, Torch!

TORCH: Get dressed!

BLUE: I wanna show you! I spent a week's salary on this. For Miss Keypunch? This represents an investment.

TORCH: What does?

BLUE: My black market street deal counterfeit decal.

TORCH: This. Is gobbledegoo.

BLUE: Lower my panties.

TORCH: You tryin' to torture me?

BLUE: O K. So I'll do it. *(She lowers her panties, revealing a large "P" very like Torch's on her left buttock.)* See? "P" for positive.

(TORCH, shocked, drops sheet and slowly approaches bed.)

TORCH: You fuckin. Stupid—

BLUE: So even if I'm caught? I'll just flash 'em my fanny.

TORCH: Dumb shit! You got it onna *left* cheek! *Boy* P's got it onna left. Girl P's got it onna *right!*

BLUE: Oh. So peel it off. Put it on the other cheek.

TORCH: How could you do this?

BLUE: No problem. It peels off.

Alan Bowne   7

TORCH: Then a squad guy could peel it off!

BLUE: Those paranoids? They might get their fingers infected.

TORCH: Don't joke *about* it!

BLUE: So would you please peel it off? In case I'm caught?

(Beat. Reluctantly, hungrily, TORCH descends to bed. Starts carefully peeling off counterfeit tattoo)

(BLUE murmurs with pleasure.)

TORCH: I don't wanna tear it.

BLUE: *(Turned on, but trying to maintain composure)* Does it. Look. Like yours? I never saw one before.

TORCH: When I was waitin' my turn? To get mine? I saw lots of guys get...get labelled, they call it. *(Peels it off; snaps her panties back in place)* It's off. *(Regards decal)* It's pretty good, I think.

BLUE: I should check it against yours.

TORCH: *(Intent on decal)* The official tattoo got a very simple design, only they needled these tiny little squiggles in. Before they laid down the color? So it should pick up the light. For the sex detectors. *(Showing her the decal)* See? They got some shine in this too.

BLUE: *(Crouching beside him, very close, looking at decal)* Oh yeah.

TORCH: This is very excellent.

BLUE: Squiggles.

TORCH: Yeah, like little spermoids, see? It would make a very good graphic. Like for a album cover—?

BLUE: It's very sixties I like it. But, Torch, I better check it against yours. Just to be sure it's a good copy.

TORCH: *(Handing it back to her)* Don't gotta bother.
It's good.

BLUE: Better safe than sorry. Stand up and turn around.

(TORCH looks away.)

BLUE: You want I should end up hanging from a
lamppost? On 14th Street?

*(Reluctantly, he stands, his back to her. Crouching, she pulls
down the back of his shorts. Holds decal up to tattoo on his
left buttock.)*

BLUE: I dunno, Torch, yours is like. More detailed.
(Lightly caresses his buttock) It's not so. Standard.
It's got, I dunno. More character. *(She licks the tattoo.)*

*(TORCH spins around and grabs her hand; they struggle for
decal.)*

TORCH: *(Starting to laugh)* You slut! Gimme that!

BLUE: *(Holding decal away from him; giggling)* Right cheek
is for girls, left cheek is for boys, right cheek is for girls,
left cheek is for—

*(He retrieves decal, flips her over, exposes her right buttock,
and spanks it on with the broad flat of his hand.)*

TORCH: *(As he spanks, laughing)* I'm! Gonna teach you!
To! Behave!

BLUE: *(Giggling wildly; mock-fear)* Stop it you're hurting
me!

*(They wrestle, laughing, across mattress. Suddenly, they
quiet and gaze at each other. As their lips start to meet,
TORCH pushes her away and springs to his feet.)*

TORCH: You're a negative and I'm a positive!

*(Beat, as he crouches on floor; back to her; and she slumps in
despair onto mattress.)*

BLUE: I know that.

TORCH: Just lickin' me on my butt like that. This shit is in all the excretals of the body. In my spit? In my sweat? Which is why even a *Trojan* won't protect you! One little abrasion on your skin? And it gets inside of you. No! Intimate! Contact! It's not just smart, it's the law. I got nothin' to do over here but read up on this and I'm tellin' you. You shoul't'nt even be touchin' me.

(Beat)

BLUE: Remember when we first met?

TORCH: So?

BLUE: Remember?

TORCH: Yeah, I remember! *(Beat)* The Sphinx.

BLUE: The Club Pyramid. And how we joked about it? Should we fuck, maybe we shouldn't, and we'd go out and play around and debate this? Places we might do it? When it was safest to try? Like a coupla kids playing with fire. Laughing. Feeling each other up. And then they started those quarantine blood tests and you tested positive and they shoved you in here and it was. Over. Just like that. Most girls? Would of felt lucky they didn't fuck you. My friends, they said you should feel relieved, you were lucky you didn't fuck him. That Torch was a P. Didn't even have a job. *(Beat)* Torch? I didn't feel lucky. *(Beat)* I just felt. Dead.

TORCH: Blue? You gonna live a natural long life. You gonna die in your sleep, with no pain. Or maybe. In a accident. Quick. Clean. No lesions, Blue, are gonna come onto you. And eat you alive.

BLUE: I dream about you. I lay on my bed and I finger myself right into that sex detector. I leave all the lights on, too. Believe it, some computer is getting a scannerful.

TORCH: *(Snickering)* Yeah.

BLUE: I just dream about you.

TORCH: Jerking off is legal. You should use your V C R.

BLUE: *(Disdainfully)* I tried.

TORCH: They got some good porno on there!

BLUE: You're not in any of 'em!

TORCH: A dick is a dick is a cock is a penis!

BLUE: Yours is special!

TORCH: Fuckin' you only saw it that once!

(Beat)

BLUE: *(With a chuckle)* We came close that time, huh?

TORCH: Did we ever. And right the next *day*! They closed off Central Park.

BLUE: What was they gonna do? Put detectors in all the bushes?

TORCH: *(Laughing, rummaging in cans.)* You want some can grapefruit? It ain't cold but— *(Finds can, opens it)* You know the thing I could never stand? About them pornos? *(Drinks from can)* Was that you knew that everybody on there? All those pretty bodies? Was like already dead. Or sixty-five pounds and cacking. *(East Coast slang for "dying")*

BLUE: *(Stretching out on mattress)* You think, back in the old days? I coulda been a porno star?

(He pauses, staring at her.)

TORCH: Yeah.

BLUE: *(Reaching out for can)* Sure, I'll have some.

(Staring, he hands her the can. She smiles at his fixed gaze and starts to drink.)

(Suddenly, he slaps can out of her hand.)

TORCH: *Don't do that!*

BLUE: *Do what???*

TORCH: Jesus, I almost forgot.

BLUE: What's wrong?

TORCH: I told you! It's in my spit!

(He turns away, crouching on floor.)

(Beat)

BLUE: Torch, I don't care anymore.

TORCH: *(Disdain)* Oh. You don't care.

BLUE: There's no *life* out there!

TORCH: No life. Out *there*. But we got lots of that in here.

BLUE: It's *my* risk!

TORCH: *(Abruptly standing; facing her)* Oh right! And I? Got nothin' to say about it! If I infect you? And *you* die? And I'm left here? A carrier? With insects in my blood like fuckin' bullets I shot into you? Then I would find a way, Blue. To off *myself*. As slow. And as ugly. As the way I offed you.

(Beat, as he turns away again)

BLUE: *(Eagerly)* The first thing is to get you outa here. I got in. We can get out. Out to Jersey!

(He reacts with disdain.)

BLUE: I mean, where it's nice New Jersey.

TORCH: Checkpoints at all the bridges! I got no N-card. They'll make me pull down my pants, take one look at my ass, and shoot it.

BLUE: They got N-cards you can buy. Cost a lot, but—

TORCH: I coul't'nt even take a *shit* out there wit'out some detector flashin' on my ass! At *some* point. In

every day of your life? You gotta drop your pants.
So save your money.

(Beat)

BLUE: So. This is it. We're stuck here.

TORCH: No. *I'm* stuck here. You can go wherever.

BLUE: *(Lies back, languidly)* Do you dream about me?
Torch?

TORCH: The fuck does that matter?

BLUE: We could be this V C R for each other. We could
just. Touch ourselves. And look.

TORCH: No.

BLUE: You can't die from looking!

TORCH: I don't trust myself! I might—

BLUE: Trust *me*! *(She rises and approaches him.)*
Don't worry. I'll keep it safe.

*(He crosses away, sits at foot of bed. She pursues,
crouching before him, caressing his knee.)*

TORCH: If only—

BLUE: What?

TORCH: If only you could shoot into *me*. Fill me fulla
yourself.

BLUE: *(Fingers lightly straying up his leg)* 'Til I spill out of
you?

TORCH: I never said this. To no girl ever. In my whole
life. I can't shake you, Blue. I can't even whack off
unless I— *(Hesitates, as her fingers stray further)* I think
about myself *hurting* you. Makin' you. Cry.

BLUE: That's nice. I like that.

TORCH: But I mean *good* pain, you get me? To just blow
all this away—

BLUE: With a scream.

TORCH: Yeah.

(Her hand has wandered into his shorts. He grabs it in hammerlock, turning it over, searching it.)

BLUE: *What are you doing?*

TORCH: Lookin' for breaks in your skin! You can get infected touchin' me there!

(She yanks hand away and leaps to her feet, crossing away from bed.)

BLUE: *Jesus! (Beat)* I gotta go. *(She rummages on floor for dress.)*

TORCH: No, don't go. We got time.

BLUE: *(Picking up dress; struggling with it, enraged)* Time for what?

TORCH: To talk. To be wit' you—

BLUE: What's the point?

TORCH: I just wanna look at you!

BLUE: I'll send you a snap.

(He crosses to her, rips away dress and grabs her.)

TORCH: You know what I hate about bitches???

BLUE: *(Struggling against him)* Take your hands off me!

TORCH: They hang out wit' you and go I am totally more than my cooz, so fuck off and relate to my beautiful brainpan and *then—*

BLUE: Lemme go!

TORCH: *(Shaking her)* If you just wanna talk and be heady and responsible? She spits on you and does *birdcalls!* Wit' her *cooz!* In your *face!*

(He deposits her on a pile of pamphlets; then he turns away; squats; eats out of a can.)

(Beat)

BLUE: *(Glumly)* That. Is a projection. Of your own inability. Of communication.

TORCH: *(Stuffing his face)* You come here to torture me. You? Are twat-average.

BLUE: *(Springing to her feet)* I am *not*! Like these other girls you been with.

TORCH: *(Rising to face her)* Bitches? *Are torture chamber jokes of some sicko Godhead!*

BLUE: Sure, those girls you hung out with. But I! Am a cut above this.

TORCH: You are basically! The same bitch.

BLUE: I am very. *Very!* Distinct!

TORCH: Your mothah!

BLUE: From these *sluts* you dicked—

TORCH: Yeah?

BLUE: And are now gonna *die* from!

(Beat)

TORCH: Oh. Thanks.

(He turns away, kicking his way through debris to window. BLUE raises, then drops, her hands, crestfallen.)

(Beat)

BLUE: You want I should cook you something? They got a stove in here?

TORCH: *(Peering out window; flat)* No. They give you cans only.

BLUE: Shoulda let me know. I coulda brung you a hot plate.

TORCH: They ration the electricity. You get one minor appliance and a light bulb. They gimme that clock radio and they are short on light bulbs.

BLUE: Jesus, what a hemmeroid this is.

TORCH: It matters? Like you said, I'm gonna die anyway.

BLUE: *(Trying to make a joke)* You're such a bastard, prob'ly you're only a carrier.

TORCH: Oh great. I can stay here the rest of my life. Waitin' for it to show up on me.

BLUE: They'll discover a cure.

TORCH: No, they won't.

BLUE: Oh! So now you're this scientist!

TORCH: It's like the common cold, Blue. Or some flu bugs. It's a kinna virus that changes, as it goes from body to body. You can't vaccinate its ass, you can't cure its ass.

BLUE: Fucking how would you know???

TORCH: I been readin'! *(Picks up stuff on floor; flings it overhead)* The government been crankin' out so much shit on this, you could paper the Bronx. Gas and electric they don't got much of. But shit? About how you're gonna die? Is *free*! They deliver it. Like junk mail around here. I guess it saves 'em on toilet paper.

BLUE: Torch, they are spending millions of bucks on this, and a breakthrough is emanating. There's no doubt in my mind.

TORCH: Blue, half of this city? Is cacked. Or cacking.

BLUE: *(Picking up stray publication from floor.)* And anyway it's good you keep up. You never used to read. I would say like. Iranian? And you would think it was this sandwich.

TORCH: *(Pointing to publication in her hand.)* There's pictures in that one. Of lesions. In full color.

BLUE: *(Quickly dropping publication.)* So? I've seen 'em. They got 'em on posters all over the subways.

TORCH: You mean, like alongside the movie ads?

BLUE: Movies? Torch, Hollywood is toast. They got no stars left. And the ones that are still around? Are very. Heavily. Into make-up.

TORCH: No movies? Where do people go?

BLUE: All the rock clubs are closed. People got too excited they would sweat like pigs it was a health hazard.

TORCH: Don't matter, you should still go out, Blue. Wit' some negative guy.

BLUE: What for?

TORCH: Yeah, I guess you're right. You can't screw him.

BLUE: I don't wanna screw nobody.

TORCH: You know, this is the thing I don't get.

BLUE: Nobody but you.

TORCH: About this fuckin quarantine.

BLUE: You hear what I said?

TORCH: If they was so *sure*. That this bug I'm carryin? Is the thing. That lesionates you. Then *why*? Won't they let you negatives, who have *none* of this cootie in your blood. Have at it wit' each other?

BLUE: *(Exasperated; turning away and kicking off sneakers)*
They ain't sure yet what it is, you know that. It maybe
incubates and shows up later.

TORCH: Incubate! This is the key conception! I been
readin my ass off on this, Blue, and I'm tellin you.
This incubate? Is a *crock*!

BLUE: Every three months they test your blood at the
office. Just last week we lost a receptionist. And now
my boss? Is *very* worried.

TORCH: Lissen to me! The thing is, if you don't know
what it is. If you can't isolate its ass and say for *sure*.
In the very most scientific labs, Blue. Wit' all the
protocols in place and controls and shit. Then you
can't yak about this it incubates. If you can't *see* it,
spittin' up lesions under a microscope—?

BLUE: *(Turning back to him)* Then you probably don't
have it!

TORCH: In shitty vitro and cultured to a fuckin T?
Then *how*! Can you demonstrate! To the scientific
community! That it *incubates*? You know what I think?

BLUE: *(Lightly caressing his back)* Tell me.

TORCH: I think this bug I got? Is not the only factoral
(Meaning "factor") here.

BLUE: *(Same; more intimate)* What do you mean?

TORCH: It's bigger than just one thing. Blue?

BLUE: *(Working his back with fingertips)* Rmmm?

TORCH: What are you doin?

BLUE: *(Withdrawing hands)* Trying to relax you.
A little massage. Can't hurt.

TORCH: I told you not to touch me.

BLUE: I'll wash my hands after! *(Begins massaging his shoulders with a professional air)* You say there's more to it than this virus you got. So tell me.

TORCH: Feels good.

BLUE: Come on! I wanna hear this.

TORCH: O K. Virus. They say virus. You know what that is?

BLUE: No.

TORCH: It's like when you don't feel good, you go to some doctor, and he can't figure the fuck from what you got. So instead of saying, I'm this stupid ignorant doctor putz-head? He says. It's a virus!

BLUE: *(With professionally interested tones and hands)* I know, it's a disgrace. But you will be happy to hear, Torch, that nobody is going to doctors anymore. Nobody wants to know shit about what's going on in their bodies.

TORCH: Sure! Cause what can they do?

BLUE: Lay down.

(He stretches out on his back. She begins working his legs.)

BLUE: Jack shit is about all. So unless they are employed by the government on this plague? All the doctors are going out of business.

TORCH: *(Incredulous)* You mean. Like even those manicure doctor snots wit' those. Those fuckin' chicky brownstone offices onna *Upper East*?

BLUE: Closing up shop. Anyway, their rich patients left New York months ago. For the French Riviera or someplace.

TORCH: Oh sure. This lowlife virus would *never* go to the French Riviera.

BLUE: *(Straddling him; professionally working his pecs)*
Yeah, I guess they think that.

TORCH: This scarlegged virus would not fit in onna
Riviera. Can you just see it? Stretched out onna beach?

BLUE: Tryin' to get a tan?

TORCH: Wit' sunglasses? A big cigar?

BLUE: And a frozen daiquiri! *(They embrace, giggling.)*

(Suddenly, she pulls back; professional again, as she massages him.)

BLUE: So. If they say it's a virus, this means they don't
know what the hell it is and they are just fucking with
us.

TORCH: Right!

BLUE: *(Massaging his stomach.)* I suspected this.

TORCH: Viruses are the stars. Of the Rowdy Doody
Show. Which is so popular all over the medical world
today. Now, you got your parvo- and you got your
retro-viruses.

BLUE: *(Massaging deeper; impressed)* Yeah?

TORCH: And the retros invert your T-cell ratio.

BLUE: Jesus.

TORCH: They invert and revert and pervert, all up and
down your— *(Enjoying massage)* That's nice, Blue. All
up and down your cellular organization. Replicating!
Like the dancing dead! In some old 1980s monster
movie.

BLUE: *(Massaging lightly around his basket)* It's
frightening.

TORCH: But to go lookin' for *one* virus only, is a stupid.
You know what I think?

BLUE: Tell me, I wanna know.

TORCH: I think— *(Squeezing his legs together)* Don't do that.

BLUE: It's your tension spot. I went to massage school, and I know. Some people, all your stress is concentrated here.

TORCH: *In my balls?*

BLUE: *(Crisp and professional; spreading his legs.)* Spread your legs. Just *under* your balls. It's a neurovascular nexus of tension. Stress is bad for you, Torch.

TORCH: *(Relaxing)* Yeah. They say that you shoul't'nt get stressed. Is that funny? They quarantine you onna Lower East Side and say. Don't get nervous.

BLUE: It's very important you stay calm. *(Working his genitals through underwear.)* I'll be real gentle here. Now what's your idea on this virus?

TORCH: It's a. Piggy-back. Virus.

BLUE: *(After a quick, confused beat)* It's what?

TORCH: For this bug I got? To be operational?
(As she straddles him, working his pecs, he reaches up and tentatively fondles her breasts.) It gotta combine. It gotta sorta— *(Fondling her hungrily)* Get humped. Dog style. By a *parvo*-virus. See?

BLUE: So you gotta have both kinds of virus in your system?

TORCH: Right. Lemme just smell you, Blue.

BLUE: *(As he buries his nose in her breasts.)* So why. Don't they test for this?

TORCH: Lemme taste you.

BLUE: *(As he licks at her breasts.)* You should tell these people. To start. Testing on this.

TORCH: I dream about you, Blue.

(She cradles his head and begins slowly, lovingly, grinding her crotch into his.)

BLUE: *(Undulant, lost in pleasure)* They can grow babies in test tubes now. So why can't they locate. A coupla viruses. Committing sodomy. In your veins?

TORCH: Blue! Don't. Do that.

BLUE: Baby, we got our underwear on.

TORCH: That's pretty thin fabric down there, Blue.

BLUE: I'll pull away in time. We can dry-kiss, too.

TORCH: *(Startled)* Fuck is that?

BLUE: It's a new thing. You just. Rub lips. You don't French or nothin. Try it.

TORCH: I don't wanna.

BLUE: Like this. *(She brushes her lips against his.)*

TORCH: I don't like it.

BLUE: Try it again!

(She grabs his chin and brushes his lips with hers. Then they rub faces all over, slowly, sensuously, as they grind their hips together.)

TORCH: *(Very, very tenderly)* I could. Rip off your tits. Wit' my teeth.

BLUE: *(Also)* I'm gonna. Squeeze your balls. 'Til they pop.

TORCH: I'm gonna. Gang-bang you. All by myself.

BLUE: I'm gonna rape. Your tush.

TORCH: I'm gonna love you. 'Til I die.

(Beat)

(Their open lips begin hungrily to meet.)

(A loud pounding at entrance door)

GUARD: *(Offstage) Lesion Squad!*

*(*TORCH *and* BLUE *scramble to their feet.)*

TORCH: Ace the candle!

*(*BLUE *blows out candle. Darkness.)*

TORCH: *(Hissing)* The fuckers come early!

GUARD: *(Offstage)* Respond in kind!

TORCH: Where we gonna hide you?

BLUE: I dunno!

GUARD: *(Offstage)* Hey! Number two dash fifteen dash six! You in there?

TORCH: Jesus!

BLUE: I got my "P" decal! We'll show him that!

GUARD: *(Offstage)* Time for your checkup! Get to the door or we're coming in!

TORCH: *(Calling, off)* Be right there! I was sleepin'! *(To* BLUE, *hissing)* Hide someplace.

*(*BLUE *crouches at side of stage as* TORCH *stumbles in the dark for door. Climbs stairs clumsily.)*

(Door opens as he is halfway up stairs. A flashlight beam freezes him. There is the dim form of a soldier in the doorway, backlighted.)

GUARD: O K, O K. Back off.

(Flashlight beam follows TORCH *back down stairs.)*

GUARD: Drop your shorts.

(Silhouetted, back to audience, TORCH *pulls down his undershorts.)*

(The bright beam plays over front of his body.)

GUARD: Lift your arms, goddamn it.

(TORCH *does so. Beam travels from one armpit to another. Stops.*)

GUARD: What's that?

TORCH: A mole. We been through this.

GUARD: O K.

(*Beam descends.*)

GUARD: Come on! Lift 'em up! We ain't got all night.

(*We see* TORCH's *arms move, lifting his genitals.*)

GUARD: O K, O K. Come on, you know what to do.

(TORCH *turns around. Beam searches his buttocks.*)

GUARD: Fuckin' plaguey. So crack a smile!

(TORCH *bends over.*)

GUARD: What a job I got. O K, you're clean.

(*As* TORCH *pulls up his underwear the beam abruptly scans the room, darting everywhere. A crash, as* BLUE *falls over something, trying to escape the beam.*)

GUARD: Who's that?

TORCH: A hooker!

(*Beam shoots to* TORCH's *face.*)

TORCH: I got a hooker down here.

GUARD: You having a nice *vacation* in Beirut?

TORCH: See, it's like this. I coul't'nt sleep and—

GUARD: *Get her over here!*

TORCH: (*Into darkness*) Get over here. (*Beat; hissing*) Hey. Bitch!

BLUE: I'm coming! (*Beam shoots to illumine her.*) I tripped and hurt my leg.

TORCH: *You O K?*

(Beam shoots back to him.)

GUARD: What do you care?

BLUE: I'm here. I'm here.

(She crosses, limping, to stand in front of TORCH, *their backs to audience, in the glow of the beam.)*

GUARD: Never seen you before.

TORCH: She just got Q'd. Today.

GUARD: What's your number?

BLUE: *(Quick)* Three dash six dash sixty!

GUARD: Show me your label.

TORCH: Sure. She got one.

*(*TORCH *turns* BLUE *around, yanks at her panties, showing the decal, the beam following all this.)*

TORCH: See?

GUARD: Very. Very. Nice. Turn around, honey.

(She does so, adjusting panties. Beam plays slowly over her body. Stops.)

GUARD: What's that?

BLUE: Where I bumped myself just now.

GUARD: *(Puts beam in* TORCH's *face.)* Show me her tits.

TORCH: What?

GUARD: I have to check everybody. Now show me her tits.

BLUE: I'll show you.

GUARD: Him! I want him to do it.

(Their backs to audience, TORCH *lowers her bra, the beam following.)*

GUARD: Oh man. Rub them.

TORCH: Mister? What is this—?

GUARD: *(Beam shooting back and forth from* TORCH's *face to hers.)* You guys got no symptoms yet. I hardly ever see that. She's not on my list. It's after curfew. Now rub her tits, butthole.

*(*TORCH *hastily begins to do so.)*

(Loud zipping sound)

TORCH: So, Mister. Is this O K?

GUARD: Show me.

TORCH: Show you what?

GUARD: *Show me her bush!*

(Beat. TORCH, *with immense tenderness, begins peeling away her panties.)*

(Heavy breathing sound from GUARD.*)*

(Sound of a siren)

GUARD: Shit! A break-in!

(Muttered curses as GUARD *struggles with zipper, the light making crazy patterns on floor and ceiling.)*

(Siren out, beat)

(Final zipping sound)

(Beam of light shoots to their faces.)

GUARD: I'll see you two. In the morning.

(Beam disappears. Door slams.)

(Darkness)

(Beat)

BLUE: *(Exhaling)* Jesus, Torch.

(Sounds of stumbling in the dark)

(TORCH *finds and lights candle.*)

(*Lights up*)

TORCH: Get dressed. You gotta get outa here.

BLUE: (*Angry*) I'm gonna be sick!

TORCH: Oh! But me? I feel like a David's cookie!

(*He rummages on floor for her dress; hands it to her.*)

BLUE: Torch? You got a little sympathy here?

TORCH: You ain't gettin dressed!

BLUE: What's *wrong* with you?

TORCH: Wanna stick around? Be a Barbie doll?
For *soldiers*?

BLUE: Why the bum's rush? You got a kind word
for me maybe?

TORCH: Yeah: Go back to Flushing!

BLUE: (*Casting away dress.*) When I'm good and ready!

(*Beat*)

TORCH: I get it. You *liked* it.

BLUE: Liked *what*?

TORCH: Watchin me crawl for that United States
scumhole of a National Guard masturbator!

BLUE: That's a lie!

TORCH: Sure, this is a *revenge* thing for you.

BLUE: Did it ever cross your brainpan. That we could
face this shit *together*?

TORCH: So fuck it, let's just hang my balls! Over the
door! So he should know when we're ready!

BLUE: Torch, we'll be *stronger* the next time!

TORCH: Maybe he'll make you go *down* on me. And I could stand there and whistle like. Zippidy-do-dah!

BLUE: I am so sick of you.

TORCH: You! Got your head! Up your cakes!

BLUE: *(Striking him)* You rat bastard!

(He grabs her by wrists, slams her against wall.)

(Beat)

(He slaps his forehead and turns away.)

TORCH: I need some drugs.

(Beat)

BLUE: *(Verge of tears)* If I wanna stick it out here? Then I'll stick it out here!

(He turns, stares at her.)

TORCH: Oh *yeah*? *(Beat)* Let's play a game!

BLUE: *(Same)* You're on.

TORCH: It's kinna scary, Blue.

BLUE: *(Turning sarcastic)* Oh. Hey. A change of pace.

TORCH: I call this game: "The Soldier? And the big. Brave. Uterus."

BLUE: And which. Are you?

TORCH: *(Cold)* Get on your knees, honey.

BLUE: *(Smirking)* I'm gonna win this game. Lootenant.

TORCH: *I gave you a order!*

(Beat)

BLUE: *(Defiant)* O K. I'm woman enough for whatever you wanna play, Torch. *(Sinking to knees)* Are you man enough?

TORCH: Crawl.

(On all fours, she crawls to him. Reaches up to pull at his shorts)

(He whacks away her hand.)

BLUE: *(Stung)* Hey! Nipplehead! That hurt!

TORCH: Naughty naughty. You shoul't'nt make a move I don't tell you. Now beg me to fuck you.

BLUE: Torch. This is me. Your girlfriend. From Queens.

TORCH: You want it? So beg me for it.

BLUE: I am *not*! Quaking with fear here.

TORCH: *(Turning ugly)* I told you to beg!

BLUE: *Come on, Torch—*

TORCH: *(Grabbing her by chin)* Beg me for it!

BLUE: *(Struggling to free herself from his grip)* Get off!

(He has her by throat.)

TORCH: And in every drop of me? Gonna be a trillion tiny cockroaches that gonna float around inside of you and poop out their shit! *Real slow!* Into your body. For like a year? Five years? Maybe longer. And all this time you're worryin about a freckle that wadn't there before. Feelin' in your pits for *lumps*! Havin cold sweats every time you *cough*! Checkin' yourself out every hour of every day till this body you got? This body you think is so hot?

BLUE: *(Gasping)* You're choking me!

TORCH: Starts to look like what it really *is*! A wax paper bag fulla livers and turds that puts coffee stains on your underpants and snot in your water glass! *I hate my body!* *(Thrusts her to floor)* And I hate yours too, bitch. *(He steps over her, crosses to her purse. Crouches, rummages in it)* You bring me any cigarettes?

(BLUE is panting painfully on the floor, grasping her throat.)

(He finds a cigarette pack in the purse; starts to rip it open, stops.)

TORCH: You believe this? They still got that sucky warning onna pack. "The Surgeon General..." Is *dead*! Of the plague. *(Rips out a cigarette, rummages for match)* Fuckin' asshole. Prob'ly thought, *I'm* healthy. I never smoke. I have nice clean sex too. We're very responsible up here. I never muffdive my wife. Mainly? I jog! I eat alfalfa sprouts I avoid salt I— *(Exploding; casting purse away)* Where's a fuckin match???

(Beat)

BLUE: *(Flat)* Use the candle.

TORCH: Oh, right. *(He crosses to candle; lights up from it. Inhaling)* Unfiltered Camels? Are the greatest invention. Of American history. *(Exhaling)* Is what I think.

(TORCH throws himself onto mattress.)

(BLUE manages to rise to her feet. Looking away from him, massaging throat, she crosses to sink; wets lips.)

BLUE: *(Strained)* The Plasmatroids? Got a. New album out.

TORCH: Any good?

BLUE: Coupla cuts.

TORCH: They only play that one cut on the radio.

BLUE: Which one?

TORCH: "Beep. Beep. You're Dead."

BLUE: *(Towelling her face with stray rag)* There's a hotter one. "Pneumocystis Carinii Killed My Dog." Heavily metallic, but with a jazz riff double-tracked.

TORCH: I miss my stereo. I miss my earphones.

(She crosses to purse, crouches, extracts cigarette, easily finds a match, lights up.)

(Beat)

BLUE: *(Eagerly)* Maybe I got it too!

TORCH: Maybe you do. But far as they can tell? From blood tests? You don't. So far you're safe.

BLUE: Safe from *what?*

TORCH: Don't be a asshole.

BLUE: *(Looking around)* Anyway, I like it here. *(Wandering about)* You can do anything you want here. Nobody cares. Nobody's watching.

TORCH: They got some pretty horny guards here, you may have noticed.

BLUE: I know how to handle him!

TORCH: You was scared shitless of him!

BLUE: Don't *worry* about it! I got a plan for that guard. The thing is, I like it here. It's a hole, but we could fix it up. We could requisition some curtains. There's an old armchair in that lot over there—

TORCH: *(Sarcastic)* Hey! Let's set up house and have a baby!

BLUE: So fucking why not???

TORCH: Who at six months of life? Gonna start gettin' these. Purple scabs—

BLUE: It's not a hundred percent infection!

TORCH: Almost!

BLUE: You'd make a shitty father anyway.

TORCH: Blue! I'm a major risk category!

BLUE: *(Flipping cigarette into sink)* You were always a risk! Even before this plague.

TORCH: But *pre*-plague? Nobody never. Ever. Fuckin' *died* from some sucky love thing. You maybe got hurt,

but you got over it. Now you put on your dress and
you get your ass outa here. You go back and—

BLUE: And what?

TORCH: I dunno! Whatever. You get into somethin!

BLUE: Macrame?

TORCH: This is not my problem.

BLUE: My job! I could get into my job. Last week? We
tabulated accounts. For a Filipino dry cleaners. Torch!
I never saw the *beauty* in this before—

TORCH: You live, that's all! Whatever that means, you
live.

BLUE: You can't *live*! Without love. You just. Can't.

TORCH: Lotsa people! *They* live. Wit'out *once*! Lovin' one
shitty flick on this planet—

BLUE: *So?* They are walkin' around dead!

TORCH: Priests, what about them? Never *once* can they
flick—

BLUE: Priests love God!

TORCH: So love God!

BLUE: I love *you*! *(Beat; as she kneels on bed)* You can't live
without it, Torch.

*(TORCH springs from mattress; flips cigarette into sink and
strides about room as:)*

TORCH: This? Is a canary! Before I met *you*? I ditn't
love *nothin'*. And I was O K. I could take it or leave it.
I walked around, hadda coupla beers, hung around at
O T B, told funny stories to the unemployment, and
then. At night? I would go to some club and lissen!
To this cunt over here? Or that cunt over there? Drool
at me about this *love* intestine! And I would laugh. And

then fuck her. Or not fuck her. It ditn't matter. I was
happy.

BLUE: You were dead.

TORCH: *(Ignoring her; lifting shade at window.)* Jesus!
If I was blood-negative? I would be out there, breathin'
so free. Who needs *sex*? I would go. To a ball game.
I would flash my N-card so casual and get on that
subway take the B M T over the Manhattan Bridge to
Brooklyn. The city looks great from that bridge. Or
maybe I would go to like Bensonhurst? You're Queens,
you don't know. But me, I'm Brooklyn Italian and
Bensonhurst? Is great! These old Italian guys? Hangin'
out in front of gelati cafes and watchin the girls—

BLUE: In shapeless sacks.

TORCH: Don't matter! *Cugines? (Meaning buddies or
regular guys of the Brooklyn streets. Based on Italian,
pronounced "koo-sjeens.")* Got X-ray vision! And the
goomadas *(Phonetic Italian for grandmothers; accent on
second syllable)* and the baby carriages—

BLUE: Babies? Torch, they kill you out there if you get
pregnant.

TORCH: *So who needs kids?* Fuckin' brats, they can raise
'em in test tubes now! I heard it onna radio! Big
breakthrough. Culture the race in jars or some shit.
No exchange of virulous fluids!

BLUE: *So who wants to be born in a petri dish?*

TORCH: So there's baseball and stickball and 86th Street
Brooklyn! Everybody on that street, boppin' around,
flirtin', eatin' take-out—

BLUE: *Nobody!* Is boppin around out there, Torch. No
stickball. No flirtin. No life. Don't you get it? Without
love to look for? Without sex at least? There's nothin'.

TORCH: *There's pizza! (Beat)* Now just. Get outa here. You make me. Sick.

BLUE: Right. My body is this bladder sack with turds floatin' around in it. I heard you. Now if you don't get over here. And fuck the stuff outa me? Within the next say twelve minutes? I. Am gonna pee. On your mattress.

(Beat)

TORCH: What if you die from it, Blue? And I gotta live with that?

BLUE: Come over here.

TORCH: Answer me!

BLUE: Come over here and I'll tell you.

TORCH: Tell me from there! I wanna hear this. How I. Can sit here. And watch those nice little tits of yours? Shrivel up like raisins. Sit here and watch you lose like fifty pounds in twenty-four hours. While your *head!* Puffs up! To twice its size! And that I done it to you. This I wanna hear.

(Beat)

BLUE: You want pizza? You got pizza. With this decal I can sneak out and sneak in. You want stickball? You got it. Wanna get drunk? Wanna nice t-shirt? It's all yours. And if one of us starts to die? Then a light meal, a glass of wine, and four grams of seconal. (Beat, as he stares at her.)

BLUE: Two grams apiece. We could go to sleep in each other's arms. Naked. So the guard should get off on it.

TORCH: *(Staring)* You gonna get serious? Or what?

(BLUE stretches out and smiles.)

BLUE: I *am* serious. You really like my tits? I never thought you did. My ass maybe, but—

TORCH: I could really see this. Oh sure. You and me playin' house in here. On Sundays we take a little stroll inna park. You seen Tomkins Square lately? It's where they pile the bodies. And burn 'em on Sundays. We could walk around, sniffin' the fresh air. We could watch the people who can't control themselves? Squattin' in the gutters wit' the shit runnin' outa them like rusty tap water. Or! We could go to the laundromat on Avenue A? And watch people tryin' to unglue the t-shirts from their sores to wash 'em. And then! Come back home and *fuck*! Wit' two water glasses and a killer dose of reds in this little *altar* next to the bed! *(Nods madly.)* It's the American Dream!

BLUE: I usta think that too.

TORCH: *Think what?*

BLUE: That life was over here, and death was way over there. That they don't mix. But *now*? They're joined at the hip.

TORCH: What we need here! Is some adult maturity!

BLUE: It's a lovely thing you're feelin' for me. How you don't wanna infect me and all? But stick it up your ass, *all right?*

TORCH: I ain't lissenin' no more!

BLUE: Because I got two choices. First, I can live without risk and feel dead. Or second? I can risk death and feel alive. *I would not be the bitch that fell for a prick like you if I would choose the first!*

TORCH: *I never liked your tits!* Very seldom. Do you find a decent pair of tits.

BLUE: Yeah? Well, *testicles?* Are a turn-off!

TORCH: Either they got cow udders or pimples!

BLUE: And I bet that *you*! Got the kinna testes that flap against a girl's ass when you fuck her! Whap! Whap! Whap!

TORCH: Tits that are nice and firm and just the right size—?

BLUE: It drives you crazy! Cold wet dog balls beatin' time on your ass—

TORCH: *Suicide!* Is a sin! It's anti-nature. Un-Italian! And non-American!

(He crosses to sink, grips it, not looking at her. During following, she rises from mattress and approaches him; finally, she begins caressing his back.)

BLUE: You had a choice about gettin' this disease? Or you had *one* word to say about *one* thing that has happened to you in your whole life, including you got born? No. It was always other people or god or some shit that made your choices. You ain't owned *one* minute of your life, Torch. But that moment you die? You can choose it. You can choose when, you can choose how. You *own* it, Torch. You don't wanna give me a baby? O K. Then give me that moment. That moment when we die. It will belong to us, Torch, and to nobody else.

(Beat, as he feels her body on his back. He breaks away, crossing to radio.)

TORCH: You wanna lissen to some music? *(Twirls dial)* Popular? Classical? Jazz?

BLUE: All I'm sayin', is it don't have to be a sin!

TORCH: *(Abandoning radio.)* You end up in hell!

BLUE: Oh my god! *(Looking about in mock-terror at sleazy room)* How will we *handle* it?

TORCH: Shut up! *(Grabs sheet, covers himself with it)* And go home. *(Huddles on bed under sheet)*

BLUE: *(Sitting on mattress.)* So. That's settled. I'm gonna get curtains for in here. And as for that guard? I know what to do about *him*. Got the idea from this T V program they showed the other night, N B C, coast to coast, about plagues like in Europe hundreds of years ago? This was supposed to make us. Feel *better*? I dunno. Anyway, they told how the people who got the Black Death? A more Christian disease than what we got now, I mean you died in a matter of mere days. How these people who caught it got very pissed off about the ones who didn't catch it. So the sick ones would sit by their front windows until well persons passed by on the street? And then suddenly reach out! Grab them! And *breathe* into their faces! People. Never. Change. *(Beat; chuckling)* So that's what I'll do to that guard. When he's good and hot, I'll ask him to come closer. And then *breathe* on him!

TORCH: *(Under sheet)* This thing here is not airborne! It's a fluid transmission only!

BLUE: Thank you, doctor. *So I'll spit on him!* We can always scare him off, scare him so bad he'll stop bothering us. There's power in being sick, Torch.

(Beat)

TORCH: Blue?

BLUE: Yeah?

TORCH: I got a hard-on.

(Beat)

BLUE: Me too.

TORCH: But the thing is, you can't have it.

BLUE: Come out from under there. I want you to look. In the candlelight? There's these little specks floatin in the air. Little animals just waiting. To kill off the things that get weak. They float and turn and dance in the light. Come on. Look.

TORCH: *(Still under sheet)* No.

BLUE: O K, so here comes a microbe!

(She gets under sheet with him; we see only their forms under it, rolling about.)

TORCH: Stop it!

BLUE: I'm a germ! I'm gonna kill you!

TORCH: You can't *do* this!

BLUE: Call out the National Guard!

TORCH: You gonna haveta do this, Blue, all by yourself. *(Big, emphatic)* It ain't. My. *Responsibility!*

(Beat, as their forms freeze beneath sheet.)

BLUE: You dickless dink. Of a cop-out.

TORCH: Huh?

(BLUE whips away the sheet and stands up over him, enraged.)

BLUE: I bet you been tellin' that to girls. *Your whole life!*

TORCH: *(Sitting up.)* The fuck is that suppose to mean?

BLUE: Men? Are *pussies!*

TORCH: Who?

BLUE: Always like— *(Sarcastic macho mimicry)* She *begged* me for it! Wadn't *my* fault if she got hurt! The stupid cooz!

(TORCH grabs her and pulls her down onto mattress; rolls her onto her back; into her face:)

TORCH: Hey. Bitch! You wanna get lucky, or what???

BLUE: *(Struggling beneath him)* I can just see you! If I come down with this? You gonna be crawlin' around here goin. It wadn't *me*. *She* asked for it. I was just this. Innocent bystander!

TORCH: Jesus, I never met such a fuckhead! So we won't do it! So get outa here!

(She flips him over; into his face:)

BLUE: You say it.

TORCH: Say what?

BLUE: That you wanna be *inside* me! *(Beat)* That what you feel, I gotta feel. That what I gotta face, you gotta face.

(Beat)

TORCH: You are some kinna fazool. Some kinna magazine. Like "Modern Romance", like "Teenage Love", like—how'd I ever fall in love wit' you? In the middle! Of a disease???

BLUE: Piss on this love you got! I don't want excuses here, Torch.

TORCH: So what *do* you want?

BLUE: I want you to climb inside me. And never leave.

(Beat)

TORCH: I get it. You want my soul, right?

BLUE: That's right.

TORCH: Typical bitch.

BLUE: That's right.

TORCH: Eight inches of dick ain't enough for you, hey?

BLUE: *(Contemptuously) What* eight inches?

TORCH: Give or take a centimeter!

BLUE: Good-bye. *(She angrily rummages in debris for her dress.)*

TORCH: Fuckin' how can this be? You love somebody and don't wanna give 'em a disease? And that makes you this. *Sonofabitch?*

BLUE: *(Pulling dress over her head)* Pre-plague? You woulda said, Hey you! Wit' the face! You gettin all hung-up and hurt here? So it's your *own* fuckin fault, you chee-chee! *(Slang for cheap girl)*

TORCH: It's not the same!

BLUE: *(Smoothing dress; grabbing up purse; rummaging in it)* It's the same.

TORCH: Bitches in a plague? Are sows in shit!

BLUE: *(Throwing packs of cigarettes at him.)* Here's some extra cigarettes. *(Again rummages in purse.)* And somewhere. In here. I brung you a Mars bar.

TORCH: Under your thumb, that's where you want us. In a fuckin' cage which only you got the key! Well, lemme tell you, wit' a guy? It's different! He wants a good time, a nice fuck, a few laughs, and then. He wants. To go out. *And play some pool!*

(Beat, as she pauses, looking at him.)

BLUE: What. Are you talking about?

TORCH: We'd be trapped here! Lookin' for spots on each other alla time. I can't live inside of you, Blue, in some kinna romantic magazine. Even if I forget and drink outa the same glass as you? Much less fuck you? I would hate myself.

BLUE: Guys always do.

TORCH: Do *what?*

BLUE: Hate themselves after fucking. You guys can have this Fourth of July experience up a woman's vage and still feel like total shit afterwards. Why is that?

TORCH: You keep changin'! The subject!

BLUE: The subject! Is you got no *balls*!

TORCH: Fuckin' *what*? I don't wanna *murder* you!
Is that O K?

BLUE: No, I won't eat that.

TORCH: It's the truth!

BLUE: I gotta go.

TORCH: What, I'm some kinna limp! wimp! Cause I
don't wanna fill you fulla parvoviroids?

BLUE: *Shit on this virus mumbo!* What you don't want.
Is *me*. A human being on your hands who might feel
pain. Or make a demand. Or need you in her guts when
there's nothing left.

(Beat)

TORCH: That! Is totally. And complete. *Bullshit!*

BLUE: Torch, I didn't risk my life to come here for a
visit! I came to live with you, maybe even to die with
you. I didn't know what I'd find. Would your skin be
smooth and white, like before, or would you be covered
with sores? I didn't know. And I didn't care.

(Beat)

TORCH: *(Pleading)* Blue—

BLUE: I know. It's like I said. *(Turns to ascend stairs to
entrance door.)* You're a pussy.

TORCH: *(Springing to his feet)* You eat that!

BLUE: Die alone.

(He crosses quickly and grabs her.)

*(A significant beat as he looks into her face, makes his
decision, then flings her back onto mattress.)*

TORCH: All right. Take off your dress.

BLUE: You take it off.

(He rips the dress from her body and grabs her between the legs.)

TORCH: You talk pretty hot for such a dry hole!

BLUE: You man enough to get it wet?

TORCH: Maybe I don't *care* if it's wet.

BLUE: Hey! Use the *palm* of your hand! What am I, a video game?

TORCH: Oh, so *now* you're gonna tell me how to give satisfaction!

BLUE: You gotta tell men everything!

TORCH: There ain't gonna be no love in this, Blue!

BLUE: *Love?* You hide behind it, anyway.

TORCH: I'm a loaded gun, Blue!

BLUE: So shoot me!

TORCH: I got poison fangs, Blue!

BLUE: So bite me!

TORCH: There's *death* in this, Blue!

(Beat, as they stare into each other's eyes.)

(She grasps him by the back of the neck and draws him down to her for a long, deep kiss. They begin making love as:)

(The lights dim.)

CURTAIN